Mandala
Peace Coloring Book

Copyright: Published in the United States by Nancy McCowan
Published January 2017
ISBN-13: 978-1542631266
ISBN-10: 1542631262

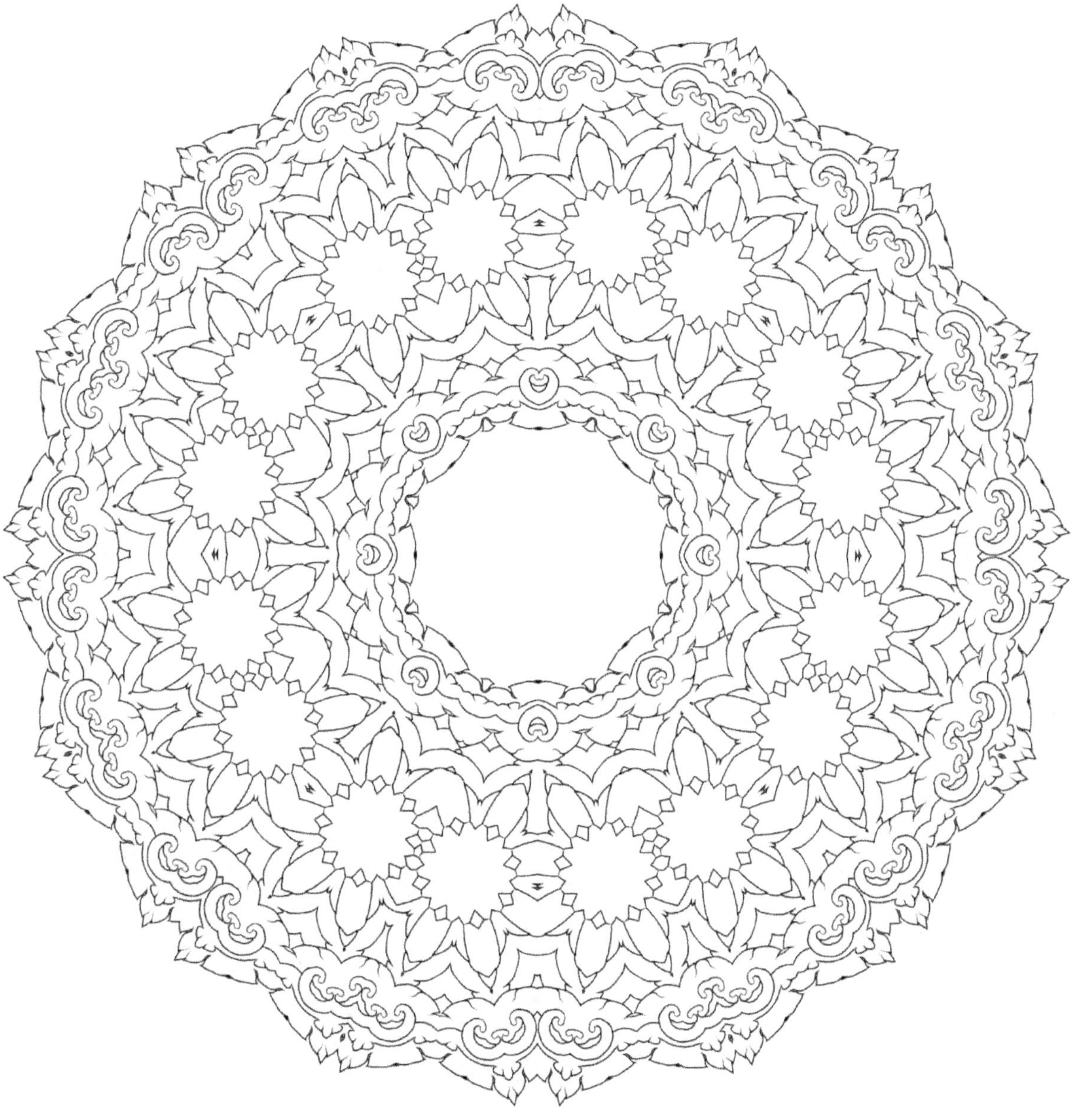

Thank you

www.ingramcontent.com/pod-product-compliance
Lightning Source LLC
Chambersburg PA
CBHW081556280526
45788CB00011B/3482
* 9 7 8 1 5 4 2 6 3 1 2 6 6 *